50 YEARS of grace

50 YEARS *of* grace

ROGER ELLSWORTH

CALVARY PRESS PUBLISHING

Published by Calvary Press Publishing.
Visit us at: CalvaryPress.com
ISBN 978-1-879737-80-8

PRINTED IN THE USA

Dedication

To God the Father, God the Son and God the Holy Spirit, who loved me, saved me and put me in the ministry.

Contents

Introduction

Fifty years in the gospel ministry! I can scarcely believe it! The years have come and gone so rapidly! I still remember the eleven year-old who stood with fear and trembling on the night of February 21, 1960, to preach to a village church, but the image is a bit fuzzy.

I definitely remember my text: "… without the shedding of blood, there is no remission" (Heb. 9:22).

There must have been no more than twenty present; although I have met at least thirty who assured me that they heard my first sermon!

I do not recommend that early of a start for others. I can only say that it was necessary for me. I had a strong sense of calling that I could not dodge or dismiss. The fire to preach burned within, and it still does.

I offer the following chapters to my fellow-ministers and to believers in general with the hope that they will provide some encouragement and insight. I will be especially glad if they help a few young pastors keep their eyes "on the ball," that is, on the gospel of Jesus Christ.

This is not an account of my ministry: where I served and what I did. It is certainly not an account of my successes. There have been too many failures for that! It is rather an assessment of some things from the vantage point of one who has been privileged to minister longer than most. My longevity has enabled me to see some mega-shifts in church life and ministry, many of which are not good.

I share my perspective on some things with a profound sense of gratitude to God for being faithful to me even when I have not been faithful to him. I am also grateful to the person God put in my life over forty years ago. Sylvia has been a constant encouragement and comfort. I also appreciate the many wonderful believers I have met along the way who have helped me in countless ways.

"And how shall they preach unless they are sent? As it written:
'How beautiful are the feet of those who
preach the gospel of peace,
Who bring glad tidings of good things!'"
–Rom. 10:15

"There is no nobler calling than to serve God as a preacher of the divine Word."[1]
–J.I. Packer

"… it appears to me to be the noblest aim in life to live entirely devoted to the one object of bringing others to know Him who has accomplished so much for us. When weighed against the hereafter, earth and its careers sink into insignificance."[2]
–F.B. Meyer

1
Setting out

My dad was a common, ordinary man who loved God, his family and his church. When he discovered that he had a boy-preacher on his hands, he determined that he would do all he could to help. I'm sure that he and my godly mother frequently prayed for me. I know that they often talked with me about the Scriptures.

One of the most helpful things that my father did was to purchase for me an eight-volume set of the sermons of Charles Spurgeon. *Sermons on Revival, Sermons on the Parables, Sermons on the Miracles, Sermons for Special Days and Occasions* were some of those titles. This purchase must have represented no small sacrifice for my parents who had very little money.

I read and re-read those sermons—and preached many of them as if they were my very own, a practice which I soon abandoned.

At the time I did not realize the importance of the theological seeds that were being planted. I assumed that all preachers believed exactly the same things, and that a sermon from Charles Spurgeon was just as good as one from Charles Finney and vice versa.

My parents studied the Word of God, but they had few resources to help them understand it. In those days, there were several radio preachers who received a hearing from my mother on most weekdays. Almost every evening, our family gathering around our old, round "supper table" would include a discussion of something my mother had heard from her favorite preachers.

The doctrines she heard on radio very much aligned with the doctrines that were preached at the little country church we attended.

So I grew up in a context which believed that salvation was part God's work (providing atonement through Christ) and part ours (believing in what God had provided). It was also a context in which as much and even more emphasis was placed on the Second Coming of Christ than his first. Practically everyone in my world took a dispensational, pre-trib, pre-mil view of prophecy, even to the point of regarding those with any other view as either being very poor Christians or maybe not even Christians at all.

In those days we were told to hold the Bible in one hand and the newspaper in the other so we could see the "signs of the end" mount up. In 1960, the two "infallible" signs of the end were the United States' early attempts at space exploration and the candidacy of a Roman Catholic for the presidency.

Being convinced that the coming of Jesus was very near, I was both happy and sad. The sadness stemmed from the fact that I had been called to preach and would have such a short time to do so. It made me wonder why God had even bothered!

As I made my way through the early years of ministry, some assured me that there would be no need for me to seek a seminary education. The coming of Christ was so near that it would be pointless!

I did my own share of preaching on prophecy in those early years, and I preached a lot. Having a boy-preacher around created quite a stir in my area. I soon had a full schedule of "supplying" for pastors and preaching in "youth rallies" and "revival meetings."

"Faith, like film, is developed in the dark."[3]
—Adrian Rogers

"When I turned from being agnostic, I went to Union Theological Seminary, eager for and expecting bread; but when I graduated, all that it left me was a handful of pebbles."[4]
—Bishop James Pike

2
The crisis of faith

When the year 1970 came along, I had been in the ministry for eleven years and had been married a few months. I had also come to see that the Second Coming might not be as imminent as many had led me to believe.

So after graduating from college on a Friday evening, I began classes the next Tuesday in one of my denomination's six seminaries. I was ready for it! My four years of studies in history and philosophy at a secular university had brought me face to face with a militant and disdainful skepticism. My Christian faith was constantly attacked and ridiculed by professors and fellow-students. In an era in which political activism was all the rage, I was out of step. In the university setting, Christianity was generally concluded as having long since been disproved and discredited and those who still held it were either regarded with amazement or contempt or both.

I was very miserable for a while. On several occasions, I attempted to defend the Christian faith in my classes, where it often seemed to be the topic of discussion. Almost invariably a fellow-student would approach me after class, glance furtively about and say in a low voice: "I agree with you." But the very fact that those students felt the need to whisper said it all! We were definitely in an anti-Christian environment! It was to me a great irony that in a university that prided itself on tolerance and pluralism, there was little patience with Christians.

I should say that my misery considerably lessened when I finally learned that it was much more fun to pose difficult questions to the skeptics than it was to try to answer their questions. I soon found that they did not have all the answers either.

Graduation gave me a huge sense of relief. All would be different now! Seminary would give me the answers I had needed in college! Skepticism would no longer be my daily companion! Faith and spirituality would grow by leaps and bounds! My seminary career would be like a beautiful spiritual melody!

Shortly after I enrolled, I discovered that the melody had lots and lots of sour notes. To change the figure, those whom I had expected to be my physicians had themselves contracted the disease!

To be more specific, there were consistent denials of Scripture's affirmations and especially of its supernatural elements. When beginning a class on a specific book of the Bible, students would often joke that while they did not yet know the author of that book they were sure it would not be the person identified in the Bible!

I soon found myself quite depressed with the whole situation, even to the point that I considered transferring to another seminary or dropping out of the ministry altogether. To me, the issue was never whether I would be a liberal Christian or a conservative Christian. It was whether I could be a Christian at all. If the liberal teaching

I was hearing was correct, I knew I had nothing to believe or to preach. So there was nothing to do but abandon it all.

Several students were in the same dilemma, and it was often the topic of our discussion when we gathered in the cafeteria. The turning point came for me when I met one of these students in front of the seminary bookstore. He asked me if I had read anything by Francis Schaeffer. When I admitted that I had not, he suggested that I buy *The God Who is There* and *Escape from Reason*. I turned into the bookstore and found both titles. It was more than a little mystifying to me that the seminary bookstore would even carry them!

Schaeffer gave me the intellectual defense that I needed for the arguments I was facing. I devoured each book he wrote and eagerly awaited the next.

I also found help by serving as pastor in one of the local churches. As I handled Scripture each week, not in an academic way, but merely to feed the people, some of my own coldness and doubt began to melt away. Some, but not all!

A very special moment came as I was taking our congregation through the first epistle of Peter. We had worked our way through the first seventeen verses of the first chapter and came to these words: "… knowing that you were not redeemed with corruptible things, like silver or gold, from your aimless conduct received by tradition from your fathers, but with the precious blood of Christ, as of a lamb without blemish and without spot" (1 Peter 1:18-19).

Suddenly, and quite unexpectedly, the words "the precious blood of Christ" leaped off the page, and I was dissolved in tears and lost in "wonder, love and praise." The people must have wondered what was wrong with me.

It had been a long time since I had been moved by the wonder of redeeming love. It felt strange and good.

When I was in the midst of the gale of doubt and skepticism, my faith seemed to me to be something that I was holding, and I often thought I was going to lose my grip. Now I realize that my faith was holding me, and there was nothing to fear. The grip of faith is the grip of grace, and the grip of grace is the grip of God, and the grip of God can never be broken.

I still do not have all the answers that I would like. I am not a Christian because Christianity answers all my questions. I am a Christian because Christianity gives me answers that I cannot get around. Somewhere along life's journey, it occurred to me that the truth about Jesus is so strong and compelling that I could safely put my questions in my hip pocket until I enter heaven's glory. There in his presence, I expect to finally get them answered, and I expect to find that the answers will all make perfect sense. I also expect to feel no little embarrassment over allowing such things to trouble me.

I trust that by the grace of God I have learned to believe my beliefs and doubt my doubts.

"He could fairly be described as a nineteenth-century preacher born out of due time, and though he was fully aware that the older type of preaching had become suspect and unfashionable he continued to practice it and to encourage others to do the same. Combining the electric energy of the orator with the analytical precision of the courtroom or clinic, and focusing his businesslike rhetoric on the inner drama of the gracious hound of heaven capturing and changing sinners' benighted hearts, he communicated an overwhelming sense of the greatness of God and the weight of spiritual issues, and left behind him a large body of hearers, myself among them, who will forever be thankful that as a modern man, he deliberately swam against the stream and did the old thing."[5]

—J.I. Packer

3

The Lloyd-Jones factor

As I neared the end of my seminary career, many of my friends and some of my professors urged me to seek a career as a seminary professor. It probably would have been a lot less bruising! But feeling strongly drawn to the pastorate, I ignored their advice and accepted the call of a church in the village of Marshall, Illinois.

Marshall was only fifteen miles from Terre Haute, Indiana, where our church members went for hospital treatment. On my first trip to make a hospital visit, I stopped at a Christian bookstore in West Terre Haute. This was my type of bookstore. It was crammed from top to bottom with books! Those who were looking for an abundance of Christian trinkets would have to go elsewhere! After browsing for a while, I picked out a few titles and was about to check out.

One seldom knows when he is standing on the cusp of something that will forever change his life. I impulsively turned down a darkened aisle and began looking. On the bottom shelf, and barely visible, was the title: *God's Way of Reconciliation*. I soon learned that this was an exposition of Ephesians 2. I also learned that the author, D. Martyn Lloyd-Jones, had served as the minister of Westminster Chapel in London. Having read about the ministry of G. Campbell Morgan, I had heard of Westminster Chapel.

But I had never seen or heard the name D. Martyn Lloyd-Jones.

I plunged into the book as soon as I got home. It was difficult to lay it down. I read and worshiped and worshiped and read. I remember the comment I made to my wife as I read: "This is what I believe."

I loved the style. This was not the mad rush and the quick dash. It wasn't a quick devotion for busy, busy people, or "a thought for the day." This was unhurried and deliberate. This writing told me that the author believed that the truth of the Bible is worth time. The truth is to be explored and enjoyed. It is to be savored. Lloyd-Jones was offering the "grand" style, and I appreciated it so much. It was big, meaty truth about a big and majestic God.

I also loved the fact that this man was so plainly and unapologetically tied to the authority of Scripture and that he so obviously disdained the proud intellectualism of the skeptics and the giggling silliness of much that was going on in churches.

One of the main things Lloyd-Jones brought to me was warmth. I had come out of seminary steeped in arguments against liberal theology, but my heart was still largely cold. It seemed that with each page I turned, another layer of ice melted away.

After a chapter of introduction, Lloyd-Jones laid out in unflinching details the reality and scope of man's sin. There was no attempt here to soften the grim details of the apostle's sobering description of man in sin. I admired the honesty of his treatment. Sin was sin. Deadness was deadness. The devil was the devil. Wrath was wrath. Grace was grace. After being in a context in which everything meant something else, it was refreshing to find someone who believed that words actually meant what they appeared to mean.

After reading chapters entitled *Man in Sin, Original Sin, Life without God, The Wrath of God,* I came to *The Christian Message to the World.* This chapter was based on two words from the apostle Paul, "But God." Lloyd-Jones says: "These two words, in and of themselves, in a sense contain the whole of the gospel. The gospel tells of what God has done, God's intervention; it is something that comes entirely from outside us and displays to us that wondrous and amazing and astonishing work of God …."[6]

The succeeding chapters unfolded in glorious and rich details the wonders of God's wondrous redemption. I feasted and feasted.

After that initial encounter, I embarked on a mission to learn as much as possible about the man who had brought so much blessing to my heart. In those pre-internet days, it was a slow process. I also began to purchase every volume I could find by Martyn Lloyd-Jones. After reading everything that was already on the market, I would eagerly wait for word that another of his volumes had been released. Like a hungry eagle, I sat looking down on the publishing process with readiness to swoop down and snatch my prey.

I usually didn't have to wait long. Lloyd-Jones' volumes on Romans and Ephesians were steadily appearing. I read and re-read each one. It is certainly no stretch to say that this man was the single greatest influence on my ministry. To pay honor to the grace of God that had used Martyn Lloyd-Jones to bring such blessing to my life, my wife and I named our second son after him. Marty Ellsworth now serves as the pastor of a church, and the Martyn Lloyd-Jones influence is very pronounced.

I never had the privilege of meeting Lloyd-Jones. That will be one of the pleasures when I land on heaven's shore. But hanging in a place of prominence in my study is a picture of the great Doctor alongside a letter he sent in response to some of my questions. I prize this typed letter because it contains corrections in his own hand.

Helpful resources on Martyn Lloyd-Jones

Five Evangelical Leaders, Christopher Catherwood
The First Forty Years, Iain Murray
The Fight of Faith, Iain Murray
Martyn Lloyd-Jones: Chosen by God, Christopher Catherwood
Martyn Lloyd-Jones: A Family Portrait, Christopher Catherwood
Martyn Lloyd-Jones: The Man and His Books, Elizabeth Catherwood
Lloyd-Jones: Messenger of Grace, Iain Murray
Sacred Anointing: The Preaching of Dr. Martyn Lloyd-Jones, Tony Sargent

"Christ is the key which unlocks the golden doors into the temple of divine truth."[7]
—A.W. Pink

"Scripture is a unity. The Old Testament is the book of the Christ who is to come, while the New Testament tells us of the Christ who has come."[8]
—S.G. DeGraaf

"… how wondrously the Scriptures open themselves to us when we focus on the Mediator."[9]
—S.G. DeGraaf

4
Finding the center

My preaching in my early years was not far removed from that which I had heard as I was growing up. I can summarize it as "be better, do more" preaching. What we could and should be doing for God was my main emphasis.

The biblical narratives offered especially rich veins for this type of preaching. We were to stand strong against sexual temptation as Joseph did. We were to slay the giants in our lives as David slew Goliath. We were to dare to be Daniel by standing against peer pressure. The feeding of the five thousand had to do with us being willing to give our little resources to the Lord as the lad gave his loaves and fish.

God used Martyn Lloyd-Jones, S.G. DeGraaf and others to help me see that the redeeming work of God in Christ is the unifying theme of Scripture, and that we cannot claim to have adequately handled any passage of Scripture until we have connected it to that unifying theme. This conclusion is based on no less an authority than the Lord Jesus Christ himself. When he walked with two of his disciples from Jerusalem to Emmaus, he "expounded to them in all the Scriptures the things concerning Himself" (Luke 24:27).

Later on that same day, he, the risen Christ, met his disciples in Jerusalem and said: "These are the things which I spoke to you while I was still with you, that all things must be fulfilled which were written in the Law of Moses and the

Prophets and the Psalms concerning Me" (Luke 24:44).

One could never get the impression from being around many pastors today that their primary calling is to preach the gospel of Christ! There is so little of Christ in much preaching these days!

By the grace of God, I determined at some point that my preaching would be Christ-centered. I began looking at the Old Testament narratives with the conviction that every story is about God and his redeeming work. S.G. DeGraaf puts it like this: " … in every story God is the prime agent, revealing Himself through His acts as the Redeemer. The entire work of redemption can be seen in each story."[10]

The story of Joseph was no longer what we could do for God if we were just as committed to him as Joseph was. It was rather the account of God sovereignly acting through Joseph to preserve his people. It points us to the Lord Jesus, who endured far greater temptations and humiliation than Joseph so that he might open a far greater storehouse than Joseph did to bring spiritual life and blessing to his people.

The account of David slaying Goliath was no longer the story by which God gave us certain "keys" or "secrets" to killing the giant problems and challenges that confront us. It was rather God's way of pointing us to Christ, who became the champion of his people by defeating Satan, the enemy of their souls, so they, his people, could be forever free. Furthermore, Jesus' victory over Satan was secured by an even more unlikely instrument than a shepherd's sling, namely, by his dying in shame and agony on a Roman cross outside Jerusalem!

The story of David having compassion on the weak and miserable Mephibosheth is not primarily to urge us to show kindness to the needy, even though that is important and needed work. It is rather to cause us to stand in awe of our Christ who found us in our misery and helplessness, and, with immense and free mercy, seated us at his own table to feast on the rich bounty of spiritual blessings.

The story of Esther is not in Scripture to tell us what we can accomplish for God if we can pluck up enough courage. It is rather intended to picture for us what Christ does for his people as their mediator.

The account of Nehemiah is not primarily about the rebuilding of Jerusalem's ruined walls through courage and persistence, but rather a picture of the Christ who comes into the ruins of sin to grant life to his people.

The story of the good Samaritan teaches us to care for our neighbours, but it also points us to the ultimate good Samaritan, the Lord Jesus Christ, who at great cost to himself found us in our spiritual helplessness and did all that was necessary to make us well.

The problem with moralistic preaching is that it always takes us away from Christ and his doing and focuses attention on ourselves. When we do that, we find horrible weakness and plenty of reasons to be disheartened. I can never be a Noah, an Abraham, a Joseph, a David, an Esther or a Daniel. But I can rejoice in the Christ who is all of these and more.

There are, of course, practical implications that can and should be drawn from the scriptural narratives, but the main thing is to keep the main thing the main thing, and the main thing in the Bible is Jesus Christ and his redemptive work.

From that time forward, my study and my preaching of Scripture became much more satisfying and brought much more blessing to my hearers.

Helpful resources on Christ-centeredness

Christ in All the Scriptures, Don Fortner

Christless Christianity, Michael Horton

Preaching Christ in All of Scripture, Edmund P. Clowney

The Christ of the Covenants, O. Palmer Robertson

The History of the Work of Redemption, The Works of Jonathan Edwards, vol. ii.

The Old Testament Explained and Applied, Gareth Crossley

The Unfolding Mystery: Discovering Christ in the Old Testament, Edmund P. Clowney

With New Testament Eyes (2 vols.), Henry Mahan

"There is no good news like the gospel!"[11]
—Adrian Rogers

"… there's nothing more thrilling to a believer than to hear the gospel preached in the power of the Holy Spirit. It melts the heart and stirs the soul—and may even cause him or her to want, if it were possible, to be converted all over again."[12]
—Peter Jeffrey

5
The glorious gospel

The gospel is the good news of what God has done in and through his Son, Jesus Christ, to rescue sinners from their sins, to give them right standing with Himself—and to bring them to share in his eternal glory.

If I could not believe anything else the Bible says, I would accept what it has to say about sin. You don"t have to pick up a Bible to see that something is radically wrong with human beings.

The word "sin" often makes us think of such things as war, murder and political corruption, but sin is not relegated to that which we see and hear on the nightly news.

Sin is in each of us, and it is far more pervasive than most realize. Theologians have often used the term "total depravity" to describe human nature. That does not mean that we are as vile as it is possible for us to be. It means that no part of us is ever completely free from sin. If I were to put some drops of ink into a glass of water, every drop of water would contain traces of ink. So each and every part of us is contaminated by sin. Every "drop" of our lives shows evidence of the sinful nature with which we were born.

Each person could write his own commentary. Have you ever said: "I wish I could take that back?" You have given testimony to the fact that your tongue is contaminated by sin.

Have you ever said: "I wish I could live my life again?" The reason we have regrets is that we have all thought things we should not have thought, done things we should not have done, loved things that we should not have loved and gone places we should not have gone.

And the wrong things we have thought, said and done are only half the story. The other half consists of the things we should have done. We have not only done wrong, we have failed to do right.

We all have a conscience that condemns us, and it takes a lot of searing to get it to shut up.

We try to convince ourselves that we are mere animals who are here as the result of some freakish catastrophe that occurred mega-billions of years ago, but our consciences will buy it only if we wage unrelenting war on them over a sustained period of time. We try to tell ourselves that we are here because our ancestors crawled out of the muck of primordial slime, but most of us know better. Human beings are morally slimy, but it not because they came from slime.

The Bible alone tells us the truth about humanity. We were made the special creatures of the sovereign God for the high purpose of living for His pleasure and glory. But our parents, Adam and Eve, spurned their high privileges and thumbed their noses at God's command. They disobeyed his command and brought sin and death into their lives.

We don't like to hear it, but we were all there! Adam was made as our representative head. What he did counted for us all. The burden of proof rests on those who rail against this teaching. If they want to prove that Adam's act did not count for them, all they have to do is stop sinning and stop dying!

Adam certainly brought physical death into the human race, but that was only part of it. Physical death is the outward and visible token of a far more serious and central death—spiritual death! While physical death is the separation of the soul from the body, spiritual death is the separation of the soul and body from God. Spiritual death means we are alienated from God. We were made to understand God with our minds, to love him with our hearts and to choose him and his way with our wills. But sin has darkened our minds, degraded our affections and disabled our wills.

If we continue in spiritual death, we will experience death in its final and most horrific form, namely, eternal death, which is the separation of soul and body from God for ever.

The one thing we most need to know about God is that he is holy. God is not only free from the taint of sin Himself; he also must pronounce judgment on our sin. If God were to ignore human sin, he would essentially "un-God" himself. He would cease to be God! So God has expressed his justice by pronouncing the penalty of death upon sinners—death in all its forms, physical, spiritual and eternal.

God is most certainly just, but he is also gracious. His justice requires him to judge sins while his grace pleads for him to forgive sinners. The sharp question of the ages is this: How could God both carry out the penalty that he had pronounced on sin—which in its final form is eternal separation—and at the same time release sinners from that penalty. Justice demanded the former, grace the latter.

Another way to put the question is this: How can a sinner be both forever separated from God in hell and forever with God in heaven?

Jesus Christ is the answer! Before the world began, he, the Second Person of the Trinity, agreed with God the Father and God the Holy Spirit on the plan by which they would redeem a multitude of sinners to the glory and praise of God's grace.

There the Lord Jesus agreed to step into human history as a man. Why was it necessary for him to take our humanity? It was humanity that sinned, and it was, therefore, humanity that must pay the debt.

But it's never enough to say Jesus took our humanity. We must also note that in doing so he did not cease to be God. So he added our humanity to his deity. Now we have someone like no other! The Lord Jesus was fully God and fully man at one and the same time!

In our humanity, the Lord Jesus first lived in perfect obedience to God's holy law. He did not fail in one point. He never thought an evil thought, spoke an evil word or did an evil deed. On the other hand, he perfectly glorified God in all that he thought, said and did.

Surveys indicate that most people now think that Jesus committed sins while he was on earth. If he did, there would be no hope for us. If Jesus committed so much as a single sin, he would have to pay for his own sin and could not, therefore, pay for anyone else.

After living that perfect life, Jesus went to the cross to die a special kind of death. Lots of men were being crucified by the Romans in those days. Have you ever wondered why Christians point to the crucifixion of Jesus as the means of salvation from sin and eternal wrath? The reason does not rest in the mere fact that he was crucified. It rather rests in the special nature of that death. Jesus did not die as other men have died. In keeping with the agreement he made with the Father, the Lord Jesus actually experienced the wrath of God while he was on the cross—an eternity's worth of wrath for each believer! That is, by the way, the reason he cried from the cross: "My God, My God, why have You forsaken Me?" (Matt. 27:46).

The penalty of sin is God-forsakenness forever, and that is what Jesus experienced there. Three statements capture the meaning of the cross: I deserve hell, Jesus took my hell and now there is nothing left for me but heaven.

When Jesus died, the justice of God looked upon that cross and said: "I am satisfied. The debt for sin has been paid." And the grace of God looked upon that same cross and said: "I am satisfied as well. Because Jesus has received the penalty for sin, there is no penalty left for those who receive him."

God's justice and grace met at the cross and kissed each other!

There is still more. What Jesus did on the cross to take sin out of the way must be applied to the hearts of individual sinners, who, in their deadness, are unable to understand or receive it. The Third Person of the Trinity, the Holy Spirit, takes care of this. He awakens sinners from their deadness, causes them to see the gravity of their sin against God and to tremble at the coming judgment and gloriously points them to the salvation provided by the death of Jesus Christ. It is the Holy Spirit who grants life and gives faith and repentance.

While the message of God's saving love in Jesus Christ has never been popular, it seems less so these days. It seems absurd beyond measure for anyone to suggest that a Jewish rabbi dying on a cross outside Jerusalem over two thousand years ago is the means of salvation from sins and eternal glory! But that is the way God has chosen. It pleases him to have it this way. The question before us is not whether we are pleased with God's plan. It is rather whether we will accept that which pleases God.

When the eternal day dawns, the redeemed of all ages will gather in praise around the throne of God. There they will lift this mighty anthem:

Worthy is the Lamb, who was slain
To receive power and riches and wisdom,
And strength and honor and glory and
blessing!
—Rev. 5:12

On that day, there will be no quibbling about God's plan. There will be no circulation of a petition that calls for God to adjust the plan. All who are gathered there will know that God is pleased with the salvation he provided, and they will be pleased with it as well. They will be glad to be freed from the ravages of sin and the horrors of wrath. They will be glad to be saved, and they may very well find themselves exclaiming:

Happy are you, O Israel!
Who is like you,
A people saved by the Lord
—Deut. 33:29

We must not be content to worship on that approaching day. Let us worship now. And let us proclaim all around the saving love of God in Jesus.

Helpful resources on the gospel

Believers Need the Gospel, Peter Jeffrey
Foundations of the Christian Faith, James Montgomery Boice
Great Doctrines of the Bible: God the Father, D. Martyn Lloyd-Jones
The Cross, D. Martyn Lloyd-Jones
The Cross of Christ, John R.W. Stott
The Ultimate Rescue, Eryl Davies

"... people can no longer sense the sacred ..."[13]
—Donald G. Bloesch

"I sometimes think if I were in heaven I should almost wish to visit my work at the Tabernacle, to see whether it will abide the test of time and prosper when I am gone. Will you keep to the truth? Will you hold to the grand old doctrines of the gospel? Or will this church, like so many others, go astray from the simplicity of its faith, and set up gaudy services and false doctrines? Methinks I should turn over in my grave if such a thing could be. God forbid it!"[14]
—Charles Spurgeon

6

Trying to hold the center

My conviction about the importance of Christ-centeredness has put me out of step with much what goes on in supposedly evangelical churches. Out of step often means out of favor, and out of favor often means in trouble!

One of my out of step areas has been preaching. For the last several years, congregations have gravitated to a style that is heavy on practical tips and humor and light on doctrine. One pastorless church even placed an ad that called for sermons to be brief and humorous and stated that anyone who dared to preach differently should not apply!

With the awesome realities of death and eternity looming before us, it is incredibly sad that T. David Gordon could rightly refer to ministers "who are not at home with what is significant" and "who are out of touch with what is weighty."[15]

Another area in which I have found myself out of step in what is commonly called "worship." The word "worship" means "to ascribe worth to God." We cannot add to God's worth, but we can and must gladly confess the worth that he has.

A passage from Zechariah's prophecy recently leaped off the page and screamed for my attention. Having returned to Jerusalem from their years of captivity in Babylon, the people asked the Lord if they should continue practicing the fasts that they had begun in their captivity. The Lord responded in this way: "When you fasted and mourned in the fifth and seventh months during those seventy years, did you really fast for Me—for Me?" (Zech. 7:5).

I suppose it would be virtually impossible to find an evangelical who would quarrel with the assertion that worship should be about God and for God. He is the audience! But while we pay lip service to that truth, the sad fact is that much of what we include in "worship" these days is not for God. It is for us! Much of the music is not about God. It is about us and how we feel, and it is designed to make us feel even better about ourselves.

There is an appalling lack of discernment among us. Anything that is moving, enjoyable, entertaining, well attended and funny must automatically be of God, as well as anything that uses the names of God or Jesus! "Tis the day of feel-good religion!"

Much of the fault for the current situation lies with pastors who have not made any attempt to learn what the Bible teaches about worship, and who, therefore, cannot teach their congregations.

But fault also lies with so-called "worship leaders," who mistakenly assume that worship is a matter of psychology rather than theology and who see it as their job to whip people into excitement and to give them an emotional "buzz."

I have often cringed as music directors stepped breezily to the pulpit and commanded us all to smile and "have a good time" when I could see some who had very recently lost loved ones and others who were trying to cope with rebellious teenagers or trying to find the way forward after a divorce or the loss of a job. Yes, Christians have plenty of reasons to rejoice and to be happy, but we are never to let all those reasons make us forget that we are also to bear one another's burdens.

One music director would frequently chastise the congregation for being "afraid" that they would become Charismatics. Let me say at this point that my primary objection to the Charismatic movement is the very issue that I am discussing: it is more about the "worshipers" than it is about God: their feeling, their healing, their success, their wealth. It is more about getting things from God than it is about God! And it is more about the Holy Spirit than it is about Christ, which must grieve the Spirit who came to glorify Christ!

My experience in evangelical churches has made me ask myself again and again: Why is God not enough for us?

The indescribably glorious God who is perfect in wisdom and power and clothed in majesty ought to be enough for his people. The God who has plucked them from eternal condemnation should thrill their hearts.

We were made to glorify God. The Westminster Shorter Catechism says: "The chief end of man is to glorify God and to enjoy him forever."

Furthermore, we are told by the Lord Jesus himself that the supreme commandment is to love God with heart, mind, soul and strength.

John Piper has consistently pointed out that God is most

glorified when we are most satisfied with him.

In light of these things, I must ask why God is not enough for us. Why we are not satisfied with him?

I can hear the strenuous protest: God is enough for us! We are satisfied with him! But are we? Why, then, do we feel compelled to have so many "God and …" services. In my opinion, you are already wrong when you add any "and" to God in the matter of worship. But evangelical churches proudly announce their "God and country" services, and every single one I have been in has always been more about country than about God. No, I am not against being patriotic, but I do believe that there is a time and place for it, and a service designed to honor God is neither the time nor the place. Furthermore, as I have watched the United States drift more and more into wickedness and become more and more hostile to the Christian faith, I find it very difficult to understand why evangelicals seem more intent on honoring her.

We should be thankful for the blessings that God has bestowed on this nation and be grateful for her Christian heritage, but we should also remember that our Lord's kingdom is not of this world.

In the last several years, churches in the United States have increasingly abandoned their Sunday evening worship services in order to provide a venue for their attendees to view the Super Bowl. My impression about such venues is the same as that I expressed above about "God and country" services, namely, they are more about the Super Bowl than they are about God.

Pastors have defended their embrace of the Super Bowl by saying that it provides a marvelous opportunity for evangelism. They get people who do not normally attend church to come for Super Bowl night, they give a brief devotion at half-time, and people come to faith in Christ! Then it is back to the game!

I know many will attribute my opposition to Super Bowl services as evidence of a sour and crotchety disposition or to being a hopeless traditionalist, but I cannot help but think that Super Bowl services were started because church leaders did not want to miss the game to do something as unpleasant and unsavory as to worship God!

It is my firm conviction that we have allowed a lot of things into our churches that will be swept away in a moment if God should decide to visit His people with heaven-sent revival.

While I am making myself unpopular, I might as well add that I have serious reservations about the widespread use of screens during worship services. Yes, I believe they can be useful for the purpose of making announcements prior to the service, and I have no objection to posting the words of songs on them. But many are being used to show pictures of beautiful scenery as a choir, ensemble or soloist sings. I wonder if this is not perilously close to a violation of the Second Commandment, which forbids the use of imagery in the worship of God. The use of such pictures suggests that we must think of God in a certain way. The problem is no picture or sequence of pictures can accurately convey the truth about God. It is a re-play of the golden calf episode in the nation of Israel. That calf was not set up as a rival to God. It was rather intended to honor him. In those days, the calf, or bull, was a common emblem for power. Would God not be pleased with the building of a calf as a means of honoring his power?

We know the answer. Far from being pleased, God brought severe judgment on the people (Exod. 32:19-35). The calf failed to honor God in two ways. First, while power is definitely an attribute of God, it is not the only attribute. Secondly, the power of God could not be accurately portrayed by the calf because his power, unlike the calf's, is unlimited.

We are loath to admit it, but there is an elephant in the evangelical room, and he has a name—Idolatry. Satan is ever such a very subtle foe that he can have us practicing idolatry while we think we are worshiping God. When we put our nation on equal footing with God, we are guilty of "nationolatry." When we design our services to entertain people and get them to applaud us as clever performers and to get them to feel good about themselves and us, we are guilty of "selfolatry" and "laughterolatry."

The times are dark and brooding. The crying need of the hour is not for churches to focus on giving people more of what they have had in the world all week, but rather to give them something that the world can never provide, that is, the way to stand before a holy God when this life comes to a screeching halt. That way is Jesus. Those who faithfully declare him are building their ministries on the sure foundation. Those who build on anything else will find to their profound shame that they have built with wood, hay and stubble that will go up in flames before their very eyes (1 Cor. 3:10-15).

Helpful resources on worship

Can We Rock the Gospel? John Blanchard

Measuring the Music, John Makujina

Puritan Reformed Spirituality, Joel Beeke

Return to Worship, Ron Owens

The Ultimate Priority, John MacArthur

Why I Left the Contemporary Christian Music Movement, Dan Lucarini

Worship, Ernest C. Reisinger & D. Matthew Allen

"To give the Bible its rightful place
is to bring glory to God,
health to the church
and light to the world."[16]
—John R.W. Stott

"We owe to the Scripture the same reverence which we owe to God because it has proceeded from Him alone, and has nothing of man mixed with it."[17]
—Steven J. Lawson

7

Believing the Bible

The last several years have brought a mega-shift in attitudes toward Christianity in the United States.

When I began my ministry, there was still something of a Christian consensus. Even though there were multitudes who did not identify themselves as Christians, there was a general respect for pastors and churches and a general belief that they were positive influences in society.

That has all changed. A militant political and cultural liberalism that desires nothing less than a sweeping transformation of American society has led the way. Those in the vanguard of this movement regard evangelical Christianity as an enemy to their goals and desire its destruction.

The nasty truth that these folks constantly hide from themselves is that while they preach tolerance as a virtue, they have very little of it for evangelicals. In their zeal for their cause, they consistently resort to demonizing biblical Christians. One of the phrases that they frequently use to describe us is "Bible-thumping morons." The hatred of Christianity in many quarters these days is vicious and knows no bounds. A few years ago, there was no reason to believe that Christians could be persecuted in the United States. Now we must say it has already begun, and it promises only to get worse.

Christians themselves must share some of the blame for the current situation. In recent decades, we have allowed ourselves to believe that the way to change society is through political means. In the process, we have spent a good bit of our time and energy in drafting resolutions that lecture people for being sinners and in trying to elect candidates who approximate our values.

I agree that individual Christians have every right to participate in the political process. Christians can and should run for political offices, and they should know the issues and vote according to their Christian values. But the task of pastors and churches is to preach the gospel with the firm conviction that the only way society can be changed is if people are changed, and the only way people can be changed is through the gospel of Jesus Christ.

We seem not to realize that our political efforts have virtually denied the gospel. If sinners can be changed through the political process, there is no need for the gospel.

We know that God always has the good of his people at heart in the harsh and evil circumstances that he allows to come their way. We must pray that he will use the current situation to drive the impurities out of his pastors and churches and to call them back to the place they should never have left.

But what about this label "Bible-thumping morons"? Is it moronic to believe the Bible? Why do evangelicals insist on hanging on to this old book that, to modern minds, seems to have long ago passed out of relevance? Are we fools to believe this book?

There are many substantial reasons for accepting the message of the Bible. We could talk about the unity of the Bible. Over forty authors wrote its sixty six books over a span of one thousand six hundred years. Although these men came from different backgrounds and had different levels of education, they produced a book that addresses one problem—sin—and points to one solution—faith in Jesus Christ. That is quite remarkable.

We could also talk about the many times in which archaeology has confirmed details of the Bible that were at one time doubted and disputed.

To these things we can add the phenomenon of fulfilled prophecy. It is nothing short of amazing that predictions that were made thousands of years in advance can be proven to have been minutely fulfilled. One can find a full treatment of this subject in Josh McDowell's *The New Evidence that Demands a Verdict*. It is particularly interesting that McDowell maintains that the Lord Jesus himself fulfilled over three hundred prophecies of the Old Testament.[18]

Yet another line of evidence is the way in which the Bible has changed lives through the running centuries.

The story of Augustine has been recounted many times. Although he was blessed with a godly mother, Augustine lived a wayward and godless life. No matter how hard he tried, he could not break the grip of his lusts. One day he heard a child say: "Tolle, lege," that is, "Take and read." Having picked up the epistles of Paul, he read: "… put on the Lord Jesus Christ, and make no provision for the flesh, to fulfill its lusts" (Rom. 13:14).

Those word immediately changed Augustine's life.

In his book *Through the Valley of the Kwai*, Ernest Gordon tells about American soldiers captured by the Japanese in the Malay Pennisula and then tortured and starved. They were turned into a group of animals, clawing and fighting and stealing food from each other. Things got so bad that they decided to start reading the New Testament. As Gordon, a university graduate, read to them, these men were converted to Christ and, according to Gordon's testimony, the "community of animals" was transformed into a "community of love."[19]

Still further, we could consider the Bible's invulnerability against attacks. Bernard Ramm captured this point in these words:

> *A thousand times over, the death knell of the Bible has been sounded, the funeral procession formed, the inscription cut on the tombstone, and committal read. But somehow the corpse never stays put.*
>
> *No other book has been so chopped, knived, sifted, scrutinized, and vilified. What book on philosophy or religion or psychology ... has been subject to such a mass attack as the Bible? With such venom and skepticism? with such thoroughness and erudition? upon every chapter, line and tenet?*
>
> *The Bible is still loved by millions, read by millions, and studied by millions.*[20]

While the above evidences are compelling and convincing,

I have to say that the supreme reason I believe in the Bible is because of the way in which the Lord Jesus treated it. It is obvious that he accepted the Old Testament as the infallible and unerring Word of God. He put his stamp of approval on it in several ways. First, he used it in such a way to indicate that he regarded it as the final court of appeal. When Satan assaulted him with three dreadfully sinister temptations, Jesus resisted him by quoting Scripture (Matt. 4:1-11).

An on-going feature of Jesus' ministry was frequent and fierce debates with the religious experts of the day. Jesus invariably confounded them by appealing to Scripture. One of the most noteworthy of these confrontations came when the Sadducees tried to befuddle Jesus on the matter of resurrection from the dead. Jesus responded by appealing to the verb tense of an Old Testament passage (Matt. 22:23-33). That is verbal inspiration with a vengeance!

Secondly, Jesus explicitly affirmed the complete trustworthiness and reliability of the Old Testament. When he wanted to speak about the certainty of Scripture being fulfilled, he selected the smallest characters of the Hebrew alphabet (Matt. 5:17-18). On another occasion, he bluntly asserted: "Scripture cannot be broken" (John 10:35). Those words reflected a common practice of that time. One rabbi would propose an interpretation for a given passage. The other rabbis would consider the argument and would either say it could be broken or could not be broken. The former meant that the argument had flaws or deficiencies in it. The latter meant that it did not. When Jesus affirmed that Scripture could not be broken, he was saying in the strongest possible terms that there are no errors in it. He was saying that Scripture cannot be demonstrated to be wrong at any point. The implication is if Scripture could be proven wrong at one point, the whole of it would tumble to the ground. But Scripture is so sure and reliable no such proof is forthcoming.

Thirdly, and perhaps most striking of all, Jesus seemed to go out of His way to affirm those parts of the Old Testament that are most often dismissed as mere myths. Adam and Eve (Matt. 19:4-5), Noah and the flood (Matt. 24:37-39), the fiery judgment on Sodom and the terrible fate of Lot's wife (Luke 17:28-32), the miraculous ministries of Elijah and Elisha (Luke 4:25-27) and Jonah and the great fish (Matt. 12:39-41)—all were treated by Jesus as indisputable facts of history.

So much for Jesus' endorsement of the Old Testament! What about the New Testament? How could Jesus have endorsed it before it was written? The answer is that Jesus gave His disciples the assurance in advance that each part of the New Testament's writing would be supervised by the Holy Spirit. The New Testament consists of three parts. The gospels and the book of Acts are historical accounts. The writers of those books would need accurate recollection of events. The epistles are doctrinal in nature, designed to provide instruction and guidance for our believing and behaving. Those writers would need keen insight into the mind of God. Finally, the book of Revelation is at least partially prophetic in nature. Its writer would require insight into things to come.

The night before He was crucified, Jesus assured his disciples that the Holy Spirit would provide each of the needed elements. He would call things to their remembrance (John 14:26), guide them into truth (John 16:13) and even disclose things to come (John 16:13).

So no matter where we turn in Scripture, we may be assured that the Lord Jesus has initialed every page!

To me the authority and reliability of Scripture comes down to one simple proposition: if Jesus is my Lord, I am not free to disagree with him on the nature of Holy Scripture.

Are there difficulties in Scripture? Yes, but those difficulties are more of a commentary on our limited ability to understand than they are on the truthfulness and reliability of the Bible. The famed scholar B.H. Carroll testified that he had at one time amassed a thousand contradictions in the Bible, but had seen all but a half-dozen vanish as he gave himself to closer study of the Scriptures. His conclusion was that the remaining six would vanish as well if he only had more understanding![21]

B.H. Carroll would most certainly agree with these words from Joseph Hart:

Say, Christian, wouldst thou thrive
In knowledge of thy Lord?
Against no Scripture ever strive,
But tremble at his Word.

Revere the sacred page;
To injure any part
Betrays, with blind and feeble rage,
A hard and haughty heart.

If aught there dark appear,
Bewail thy want of sight;
No imperfection can be there,
For all God's words are right.

The Scriptures and the Lord
Bear one tremendous name;
The written and the incarnate Word
In all things are the same.

The thoughts of men are lies;
The Word of God is true;
To bow to that is to be wise;
Then hear, and fear, and do

Let the world deride me as a "Bible-thumping moron," I will believe the Bible and gladly join John Wesley in saying:

I am a creature of a day, passing through life as an arrow through the air. I am a spirit come from God, and returning to God: Just hovering over the great gulf; till, a few moments hence, I am no more seen; I drop into an unchangeable eternity! I want to know one thing,—the way to heaven; how to land safe on that happy shore. God Himself has condescended to teach the way: For this very end he came from heaven. He hath written it down in a book. O give me that book! At any price, give me the book of God![22]

I also take as my own these lines:

Though the cover is worn
And the pages are torn,
And though places bear traces of tears,
Yet more precious than gold
Is the book, worn and old,
That can shatter and scatter my fears.

When I prayerfully look
In the precious old Book,
Many pleasures and treasures I see;
Many tokens of love
From the Father above,
Who is nearest and dearest to me.

This old Book is my guide
"Tis a friend by my side,
It will lighten and brighten my way;
And each promise I find
Soothes and gladdens my mind
As I read it and heed it today
—Anonymous

Helpful resources on the Bible

Authority, Martyn Lloyd-Jones

Baptists and the Bible, L. Russ Bush and Tom Nettles

God Speaks to Man, J.I. Packer

God's Book for God's People, John R.W. Stott

Nothing But the Truth, Brian H. Edwards

The Foundation of Biblical Authority, James Montgomery Boice, Ed.

The Infallible Word: a Symposium by Members of the Faculty of Westminster Theological Seminary, 1946

Why Believe the Bible, John MacArthur

Why I Preach the Bible is Literally True, W.A. Criswell, Broadman Press, Nashville, TN, 1969

"The pulpit is the throne for the Word of God"[23]
—Martin Luther

"... congregations never honor God more than by reverently listening to His Word with a full purpose of praising and obeying Him once they see what He has done and is doing, and what they are called to do."[24]
—J.I. Packer

"A deaf church is a dead church."[25]
—John R.W Stott

"The Word of God is the scepter by which Christ rules the church and the food with which he nourishes it."[26]
—John R.W. Stott

8
Thoughts on preaching

If the Bible is indeed the Word of God, the preaching of the Bible must be regarded as a sacred priority. The apostle Paul writes: "How then shall they call on Him in whom they have not believed? And how shall they believe in Him of whom they have not heard? And how shall they hear without a preacher? (Rom. 10:14).

What is preaching? As far as I am concerned, it is the man of God explaining and applying the Christ-centered Word of God in the power of the Spirit of God to the glory of God so that his hearers may do the will of God.

My definition is similar to the one offered by J.I. Packer:

> *Christian preaching … is the event of God bringing to an audience a Bible-based, Christ-related, life-impacting message of instruction and direction from himself through the words of a spokesperson.*[27]

We don't have preaching if we don't have a man of God, that is, a man called by God to preach truths that he prominently displays in godly living. Of a man who was known for preaching well and living poorly, Charles Spurgeon said:

> *… when he was in the pulpit everybody said he ought never*

to come out again, and when he was out of it they all declared he never ought to enter it again.[28]

We don't have preaching if the sermon is not drawn from the Christ-centered Word of God. It is not enough to merely draw a text from the Bible. If we ask a passage the wrong questions, it will always give us the wrong answers! The Bible has God's redeeming work through Christ as its overarching theme. Each individual passage, therefore, must be approached with the overall theme of the Bible in mind. If we understand the Bible as a handbook or manual for making life more comfortable and approach individual passages in that light, we have already lost our way.

I agree with W. Robert Godfrey" observation:

The Bible is ... a progressive unfolding of God's plan and activity to save his people in Jesus Christ. The Bible moves from God creating mankind for fellowship with him, to the breaking of that fellowship through sin, to God's work to gather a people out of fallen mankind and from that people to bring a Savior into the world. Here is the great message of the Bible, and everything in Scripture contributes to making that clear.[29]

William Perkins defines preaching as declaring "one Christ, by Christ, to the praise of Christ."[30]

James Stalker was right on target with these words: "Enthusiasm for Christ is the soul of preaching."[31]

We can and should be thankful that there has been something of a return to expository preaching in recent years, but we should be concerned about preachers, in the name of exposition, producing academic sermons that are dry and dull. I fear some preachers have become overly interested in preaching textbook expository sermons. They want to make sure they touch on each phrase, and sometime each word, in a passage. It's almost as if they are preaching to other preachers or to professors of preaching instead of to an eternity-bound people.

I am also concerned about the slavish use of alliteration in expositions. I have gotten the impression more than once that a sermon had been constructed out of a concern to alliterate. Alliteration may be helpful, but it should also serve the text rather than forcing the text to serve it.

Furthermore, you don't have preaching if it is not empowered by the Spirit of God. The preacher must never rely on his education, personality, eloquence, quick-wittedness or humor to carry the day. He must never enter a pulpit without the keen awareness that all that he does is of no avail if the Spirit of God does not catch him up and carry him along. It is the Spirit alone who can enlighten minds, elevate affections and energize wills.

When the Spirit of God empowers preaching, there is a melting quality about it. We can only lament that such melting is so rare these days. At the same time we should never allow the scarcity of it to keep us from diligently seeking it.

If we are to have the power of the Spirit of God attending our efforts to preach, we must make much of Christ. Yes, we are back to Christ-centeredness again! If the Holy Spirit came to glorify the Lord Jesus, does it not make sense to say that he is more likely to empower preaching that exalts the same Jesus he came to glorify?

We must also be men of prayer. Prayer is the natural and instinctive response of the preacher who is acutely aware of the spiritual deadness of sinners and his own helplessness before that awesome reality.

Finally, you do not have preaching if the preacher does not preach for the glory of God. This means preaching must not only be done in such a way as to cause the hearers to give praise to God but also it must be done in such a way that they will be conscious of his glory. John Piper says:

> *People are starving for the greatness of God. But most of them would not give this diagnosis of their troubled lives. The majesty of God is an unknown cure. There are far more popular prescriptions on the market, but the benefit of any other remedy is brief and shallow. Preaching that does not have the aroma of God's greatness may entertain for a season, but it will not touch the hidden cry of the soul: "Show me thy glory."* [32]

It should go without saying that preachers cannot at one and the same time make God great and themselves great. James Denney observes: "No man can give the impression that he himself is clever and that Christ is mighty to save."[33]

It should also be obvious to us that true preaching is the most serious business in the world. Preaching is serious because the preacher is called to present the reality and enormity of sin, the certainty of divine judgment and the critical urgency of fleeing in repentance and faith to the Lord Jesus Christ as the only solution.

Charles Spurgeon admonishes preachers with these piercing words:

> *We cannot play at preaching.*
> *We preach for eternity.*[34]

John R.W. Stott reminds us of the seriousness of the preacher's task by writing: "A congregation learns the seriousness of the gospel by the seriousness with which their pastors expound it."[35]

He then adds the account of a preacher asking an actor why he, the actor, was able to draw huge crowds with his fiction, while he, the preacher, had only small crowds. The actor answered: "I present my fiction as though it were truth; you present your truth as though it were fiction."[36]

Neil Postman writes: "Christianity is a demanding and serious religion. When it is delivered as easy and amusing, it is another kind of religion altogether ... There is no doubt, in other words, that religion can be made entertaining. The question is, by doing so, do we destroy it."[37]

With the seriousness of the preaching task in mind, I have often found myself saying to young preachers: "You had better think about preaching, but if you think too much about it, you will never preach."

Helpful resources on preaching

Anointed Expository Preaching, Stephen F. Olford

Between Two Worlds, John R.W. Stott

Christ-Centered Preaching, Bryan Chapell

Expository Preaching, John MacArthur, Jr.

Famine in the Land, Steven J. Lawson

Feed My Sheep: A Passionate Plea for Preaching, Don Kistler, Ed.

Preaching and Preachers, Martyn Lloyd-Jones

Preaching, Stuart Olyott

Preaching: The Centrality of Scripture, R. Albert Mohler

Preaching for God's Glory, Alistair Begg

Sacred Rhetoric, Robert L. Dabney

The Passion Driven Sermon, Jim Shaddix

The Preacher's Portrait, John R.W. Stott

"It is our task to show people how to get to heaven."[38]
—R.C. Sproul

"We must never confuse our desire for people to accept the gospel with creating a gospel that is acceptable to people."[39]
—Oswald Chambers

" ... I advocate the "redemptive-historical" approach to preaching, which treats the Bible as an unfolding drama of redemption rather than as a handbook of timeless principles. ... Instead of trying to make the Bible relevant for "today's busy Christian," I suggest that we allow the Bible to arrest us, condemn us, justify and free us. We need more preaching that focuses on God and what he has done, is doing, and will do in history, and less on ourselves and how we can be happier with God's help."[40]
—Michael Horton

9
The flight from preaching

I wish preachers believed in preaching! Many do. Thank God for them! But many apparently do not. Everywhere I look in my Southern Baptist context, I see a flight from preaching. Sunday evening services are becoming increasingly rare, and many of those that remain are not given to preaching. The reasoning is that it is so hard to get a crowd together for a preaching service on Sunday evenings, that there is no point in trying. The sad fact is that many pastors are giving into their situation rather than trying to change it.

It's not just a matter of abandoning services that once provided preaching. It is possible to have a preaching service and not have any preaching! That may very well be the reason that so many have stopped attending Sunday evening services!

I believe preaching is an immense privilege, and I'm persuaded that our people sorely need it. Think about it for a moment. The general expectation in evangelical churches is that the sermon will last about thirty minutes. If we preach twice a week that is one hour! How many hours do our people spend in absorbing the things of the world? One hour is minimal for the pastor to give his hearers the instruction and application from the Word of God.

I have cited the difficulty of gathering a crowd as one

reason for the flight from preaching. There are others. It has become very popular in American churches to refer to those who lead the singing as "worship leaders." The plain and tragic implication is that worship ends when the music ends and the preaching begins! But if we understand worship to mean ascribing worth to God or exalting God, we must surely conclude that preaching is indispensable to worship. Nothing exalts God more than his people gladly and seriously listening to his word!

The current abandonment of preaching may be due in part to the fact that the word "preaching" is widely considered to imply something that is negative and unpleasant. The ultimate "comeback" to anyone who says something we don't like is: "Don't preach to me!" John R.W. Stott rightly observes: ""To preach" has come to mean "to give advice in an offensive, tedious or obtrusive manner…"[41]

Preaching has come to mean talking down to people. The word has become so unpopular that many pastors now refer to preaching as "sharing," which often appears to mean saying lots of things that will entertain and amuse the hearers and nothing that will upset them.

John Piper writes:

Laughter seems to have replaced repentance as the goal of many preachers. Laughter means people feel good. It means that they like you, it means you have moved them. It means you have some measure of power. It seems to have all the marks of successful communication—if the depth of sin and the holiness of God and the danger of hell and need for broken hearts is left out of account. I have been literally amazed at conferences where preachers mention the need for revival and then proceed to cultivate an atmosphere in which it could never come.[42]

Piper also notes: "Sometimes it seems that levity is the greatest enemy of any true spiritual work being done in the hearers."[43]

It is tragically true that we can cultivate a frivolity that undermines and destroys the gravity of the gospel.

I fear that many pastors have the wrong motive in their ministry. They would never openly admit it, but they are driven by the desire to build a religious empire for themselves. Being the head of such an empire does, after all, have its perks! A large and growing church means one is known as a successful pastor, and successful pastors make good salaries and live in nice houses. They also get invited to speak in prestigious conferences.

But it all comes with a price tag. To have a large and growing church means that the pastor must attract people and hold them. What does it take these days to attract and hold people? The pastor must be warm and likable, and, above all else it seems, funny. In American society laughter has become self-authenticating. If something is funny, it is automatically right and good! Woe to the pastor who is too serious about things!

Part of being likable is preaching a message that doesn't disturb people. Sin, guilt, wrath, hell, holiness and repentance are all out in the mad desire to give people the "warm fuzzies." Never mind that all these themes were prominent in the preaching of Jesus! What would he know about modern day audiences?

We urgently need to understand that Christianity features a body of truth so central to it that without that body or some portion of it, we no longer have Christianity. Because they have dismantled or ignored so many of those essential truths, many are in no better position than the man who claimed to have George Washington's axe—even though it had a new head and a new handle! Whatever we have left after the ditching of Christianity's truths is not Christianity.

So God has become more of a giant helper in the sky, whose primary concern is to take all the bumps out of life's road so we can drive smoothly along. He is the user-friendly God. He wants us to know how to manage our money, our time and our conflicts. He wants us to be able to blend our careers with our family responsibilities. He wants us to have our best life now! Forget the fact that this life only lasts seventy, eighty or ninety years, and in many cases a lot less. It is this life that counts! Ignore the fact that Jesus plainly said that we are not to labor for the food that perishes (John 6:27), and the things of this life are quite plainly perishing!

Many pulpits have turned God into something of a cosmic cheerleader. He sees us struggling to cope with it all, but he is pulling for us. In the Bible, he offers tips and guidelines on how to balance things, and he gives us a little extra shot of strength from time to time. And he wants us to come to church, not to worship him with a sense of reverence and awe and to give thanks for redeeming grace, but so we can get another shot of inspiration (including, of course, generous doses of humor) to get us through another week and back to church on Sunday to get those all-important guidelines, steps, keys, secrets or principles from the pastor. I'm sure people of every generation have been busy and have had difficulties in coping with life, but no generation has been more impressed with being busy and more intimidated by life's challenges than the current one. We clutter up our lives with all sorts of time-consuming and stress-producing activities, and then complain that we are busy and stressed! And pastors, anxious to please their listeners and build their careers, condone the clutter and dispense the tips!

Career-building, or as I termed it above, empire-building, is the only explanation I have for ministers who have abandoned the message of sin, wrath, repentance and salvation for the message of happiness in the here and now.

The true preacher is never able to get eternity out of his mind because God has, as it were, engraved it on his eyes.

We must try to live with a consciousness of eternity. When we look at a picture snapped a few years ago, we would do well to wonder how many of those people are now in eternity. When we survey our congregations from the platform, we should remind ourselves that some may be about to hear their last sermon and try to preach as Richard Baxter advised—"as never sure to preach again, and as a dying man to dying men."[44]

Eternity—vast, boundless, eternity—spent either in bliss

or in misery and woe! What could possibly matter more? The Lord Jesus emphatically asked: "For what is a man profited if he gains the whole world, and loses his own soul? Or what will a man give in exchange for his soul?" (Matt. 16:26).

It was Jesus who plainly said: "And I say to you, My friends, do not be afraid of those who kill the body, and after that have no more that they can do. But I will show you whom you should fear: Fear Him who, after he has killed has power to cast into hell; yes, I say to you, fear Him!" (Luke 12:4-5).

We must never forget that Jesus followed that stern admonition with the powerful story of the rich man who was so absorbed with his barns and crops that he had no time for God. He concluded that account with these terrifying words: "But God said to him, "You fool! This night your soul will be required of you; then whose will those things be which you have provided?" (Luke 12:20).

Then he added these solemn words of application: "So is he who lays up treasure for himself, and is not rich toward God" (Luke 12:21).

My advice to my fellow preachers is to preach for eternity. If you build with wood, hay and stubble, the day of accounting will reveal your utter foolishness. Preach in such a way that your hearers will emulate Bunyan's pilgrim by fleeing the City of Destruction, and, upon being urged to come back, will run headlong down the path with hands clasped over their ears, crying: "Eternal life! Eternal life!"

I can well imagine when the tides of time have finally

broken on the shores of eternity, many preachers looking back in amazement over their ministries, exclaiming over and over: "I preached that instead of the gospel!"

May God help all of us who preach to not be clothed in shame when eternity dawns, but rather be robed with glory as one who faithfully preached the gospel of Jesus Christ.

Helpful resources on the flight from preaching

Christless Christianity? Michael Horton

The Courage to be Protestant, David F. Wells

God in the Wasteland, David F. Wells

No Place for Truth, David F. Wells

This Little Church Went to Market, Gary Gilley

This Little Church Stayed Home, Gary Gilley

What's Wrong with Preaching Today?, A.N. Martin

"Many definitions and descriptions of revival have been offered but I would elaborate it like this: a true Holy Spirit revival is a remarkable increase in the spiritual life of a large number of God's people, accompanied by an awesome awareness of the presence of God, intensity of prayer and praise, a deep conviction of sin with a passionate longing for holiness and unusual effectiveness in evangelism, leading to the salvation of many unbelievers.

Revival is remarkable, large, effective and, above all, it is something that God brings about. It is quite impossible for man to create revival. Though men may prepare and pray for it, revival is the work of the sovereign God, not primarily for the benefit of the people, but for his own honour and glory."[45]

—Brian H. Edwards

10
We need revival!

The things I have described above—the lack of Christ-centeredness in our preaching and worship, the loss of confidence in the Bible as the Word of God and the ever-increasing infatuation with the world—indicate to me the desperate need for revival among churches and pastors.

During my fifty years of ministry, I have been in many, many revival meetings, but I am yet to see true revival.

What is revival? The word itself gives us the answer. The prefix "re" means "back," and the root "vive" refers to "life" or "vitality." Revival is, therefore, going back to life. It is returning to vitality.

It should be plain to us that revival is something that applies only to God's people because they alone enjoy spiritual life. We are all born into a state of living death. We are alive physically but dead spiritually (Eph. 2:1).

Christians are those who have been given life by God. We were dead toward God and unable to help ourselves. How do dead people help themselves? They don't! The good news of the Bible is this: God grants spiritual life to sinners. Christians were once just like everyone else—dead in our sins. But God came into the spiritual cemetery, found us and granted life to us (Eph. 2:1-7).

We can never lose the life that God granted us. He is the author and sustainer of it. But we can get into a state of spiritual sickness and lethargy. Just as we can have life physically and be far from being healthy and robust, so we can have life spiritually and be in a very low condition.

Revival drives out the illness and restores God's people to health again.

What does genuine revival look like? It invariably demonstrates itself in the following ways:

- an intense conviction of sin, leading to repentance
- deep humility and brokenness
- the healing of strained relationships through reconciliation and restitution
- fervent, passionate prayer
- an irrepressible joy
- a realization of the preciousness of the gospel
- a return to complete faith in the authority of the Word of God
- a refusal to put emotional experiences over the Word of God
- a profound interest in the public services of the church.

We should note that while revival pertains to God's people, it never leaves unbelievers untouched. In times of revival, there is a magnetism that draws unbelievers to the church and the things of God. Revival always features a great number of conversions. Revival is an extraordinary moving of God among his people that produces extraordinary results.

Can we legitimately expect to see a revival in these days? Many believers, I fear, would answer with a resounding "No!" Some would do so on prophetic grounds. These people often say that the next thing on God's agenda is the rapture, not revival. They believe that God intends for things to grow progressively worse so the Lord Jesus can come and the anti-Christ can be revealed. Revival would gum up the works!

My answer to this view is merely that the Bible never encourages us to use its prophetic teachings to justify apathy and carelessness about spiritual things. We do not know when the Lord is coming. We should not, therefore, rule out revival on the grounds that he will soon return. There is nothing in the Bible's teaching of revival that in any way contradicts what it has to say about the coming of the Lord.

Others dismiss the possibility of revival on sociological or cultural grounds. They argue that revival is a phenomenon that occurred in less sophisticated times when people did not enjoy all our technological advantages. People went to church in those days to give themselves something to do.

The problem with this view is that it leaves out God. While society has changed, he has not.

Then there are those who argue that revival cannot occur because our times are so hard. Apathy about spiritual things is deeply entrenched. Evil is so strong. The forces arrayed against the church are so militantly aggressive, and the churches are so weak. All of these things and more seem to make any talk of revival appear to be utter nonsense.

This view also leaves out the God who tells us that nothing is impossible for him (Gen. 18:14; Luke 1:37).

Those who think the times are too hard for God to move would do well to read the history of revival. One of the greatest examples of God's extraordinary work of revival came during the ministries of George Whitefield and John Wesley. Prior to this, England was in the most dreadful condition imaginable.

In the first of his two remarkable volumes on the life of Whitefield, Arnold Dallimore documents the moral and spiritual darkness of that time. He cites "an uncontrollable orgy of gin drinking" and "the unwonted heartlessness" which often manifested itself in "cruelty to animals," and "a deep-seated inhumanity" that had come over England.[46]

He further states that crime had become so prevalent that the authorities made 160 crimes punishable by death. But the tide flowed on unabated. Dallimore writes:

> *...the treatment of the insane, cruelties to children, the London mob—Sir Mob it called itself—the incredible extent of gambling, the obscenity of the stage—"that sink of all corruption" as John Wesley termed it—these and similar aspects of English conditions might be depicted at length.*[47]

Dallimore also cites the grim assessments of some who observed those days. Bishop Butler stated that skepticism had become so common that Christianity was regarded as though "it was now discovered to be fictitious … and nothing remained but to set it up as the subject of mirth and ridicule."[48] Archbishop Secker wrote of "the torrent of impiety."[49]

Conditions in the American colonies were no better. Samuel Blair of New Londonderry offered this grim assessment in the spring of 1740: "Religion lay as it were a-dying and ready to expire its last breath of life …."[50]

Many considered the situation to be utterly hopeless, but God moved in and did his extraordinary work of revival. J.R. Green described the effects of this revival in England:

> *… a religious revival burst forth … which changed in a few years the whole temper of English society. The Church was restored to life and activity. Religion carried to the hearts of the people a fresh spirit of moral zeal, while it purified our literate and our manners. A new philanthropy reformed our prisons, infused clemency and wisdom into our penal laws, abolished the slave trade, and gave the first impulse to popular education.*[51]

The revival that came to England and to the American colonies through the ministries of Whitefield and Wesley is by no means an isolated incident. God has frequently revived his people. In his perceptive and helpful book, *A People Saturated with God*, Brian Edwards lists 57 revivals from 1150 to 1972.[52]

Revival is still possible, but when can it be expected? The answer can be put in this way: When God's people so see the need for revival and so desperately desire it that they are willing to stop making excuses for their sins and repent, they can rightly conclude that God has already begun the work of revival in their midst.

Over the years, I have heard many sermons on revival. Almost without exception, they have begun with a litany of societal woes: crime, political corruption, permissiveness, pornography, divorce and so on.

The problem is that we can get so occupied with bemoaning the conditions of our day and in pointing fingers of condemnation at wicked people and their wicked ways that we fail to see ourselves.

We should learn from the prayer that the people of God prayed in their captivity in Babylon (Isa. 64). One of the fascinating things about this prayer is that it contains no reference to the Babylonians at all. The people recognized that they were in Babylon, not primarily because of the Babylonians, but rather because of their own sins.

The single greatest barrier to revival is this: God's people do not fervently desire it! We think we do. Let a pastor stand in his pulpit and call for revival, and his hearers will nod in agreement or even say "Amen." But what they often mean is that they want other people to have a revival. We all recognize that revival produces positive benefits for society, and we want those positive benefits. But we also know that revival is a costly business, that it will change the way we living, and we are not anxious to have the price extracted from us.

We must put ourselves in Jesus' parable of the prodigal son. We must see ourselves as having strayed from the

Father's house and having taken up residence in the far country of sin and selfishness. If we are to know revival, we must do as the son did. We must come to our senses and return to God. We must say to the Lord what the prodigal said to his father: "Father, I have sinned against heaven and in your sight, and am no longer worthy to be called your son" (Luke 15:21).

The need of the hour is for God's people to take a long, hard look at their disregard for the Lord's house, the Lord's Word, the Lord's Day and say: "I have sinned."

We must no longer be content to declare détente with filthy, irresponsible talking, with bitterness and resentment, with lustful thinking and doing, with coldness of heart, and say "I have sinned."

We can expect revival when we take seriously the words of Hosea 14:1-2:

O Israel, return to the Lord your God,
For you have stumbled because of your iniquity;
Take words with you,
And return to the Lord.
Say to Him,
"Take away all iniquity;
Receive us graciously…"

Helpful resources on revival

Can We Pray for Revival?, Brian H. Edwards

Distinguishing Marks of a Work of the Spirit of God, Works of Jonathan Edwards, vol. i.

Downpour, James McDonald

God's Harvest, I.D.E. Thomas

Give Him No Rest, Erroll Hulse

The Great Awakening, Joseph Tracy

Revival! Brian H. Edwards

Revival, Martyn Lloyd-Jones

Revival, Richard Owen Roberts

When God Moves, John Armstrong

"For our light affliction, which is but for a moment is working for us a far more exceeding weight of glory, while we do not look at the things which are seen, but at the things which are not seen. For the things which are seen are temporary, but the things which are not seen are eternal."
—2 Cor. 4:17–18

11

God tearing up life

In the fall of 2007, I sat down with my good friend David Clark to enjoy a meal and to discuss future publishing ventures. In the course of our conversation, he suggested that I plan to write a book entitled, *What the Bible Teaches about Suffering*. I readily agreed. Having been a pastor for years, I know what the Bible has to say about suffering. I have read numerous books on suffering from several great divines. I have ministered countless times to suffering people. So I could see no problem in writing such a book.

If I had known what was lying ahead of me, I would have declined. It was as if at that very moment God said: "You don't know anything about suffering, but you are about to learn."

I soon found myself enrolled in God's school of affliction. While I was still recovering from surgery, things began to unravel in my pastorate of almost twenty years. Some of those I counted as very dear friends began to agitate for my departure from the church, while admitting that I had faithfully preached the Word of God to them and had diligently ministered to them in their hours of crisis. After trying unsuccessfully for weeks to resolve the issues, I resigned with a broken heart. What were the issues? These: A different view of salvation (God-centered as opposed to man-centered), a different view of worship (majestic and

God-honouring as opposed to the "let the good times roll" variety), a different view of ministry to teenagers and children (solid Bible content as opposed to tradition and entertainment).

Another surgery followed a few weeks after my resignation. Still another surgery came mere weeks after the second.

A few weeks after my resignation, I accepted a much smaller pastorate. But my aching heart was not in the work, and I soon resigned. After years and years of what most would call a successful ministry, I found myself at age sixty, financially unable to retire and with virtually no prospects for full-time employment.

Somewhere along the way, I realized that I was in a full-scale battle against depression. Sadness became my daily companion. It got up with me in the morning and went to bed with me at night. It sat beside me when I drove my car, and it accompanied me when I took a walk. When I opened my Bible, sadness stared at me from its pages.

Physical problems, depression, a dramatic decrease in income, betrayal by friends! I felt as if I were re-living the book of Job. That book now became much more than an area of academic investigation. I was living on a smaller scale much of what Job experienced. Like him, I even had days when death seemed more preferable to me than life.

It seemed to me after living a fairly tranquil life for years that the very God I had devoted my life to serving was now my enemy. It was as if he suddenly looked down from heaven one day, saw me and said to his heavenly court: "I am going to tear up his life."

I know I am not alone in what I have experienced. Many feel that the God they have tried to love and serve is bent on tearing up their lives. The congregation of the suffering has many members.

Does God do the tearing?

Suffering ties a tight knot for us to untangle. God is supposed to be both loving enough to want good things for his people and powerful enough to change their circumstances when bad things come their way. Why, then, do his people suffer?

Some make no attempt to untangle the knot. They opt to cut it. They do so by affirming that God is very much like us in that he is not always able to achieve the ends he desires. He doesn't want his people to suffer, and he tries to protect them from it, but he oftentimes fails. We struggle with computer foul-ups and incompetent staff. It is the same with God! So we suffer, and God feels very badly about it all. When we finally come home to heaven, he will be there with hat in hand to apologize. He will tell us that he meant well, but frequently failed, and he will beg our forgiveness.

Some may find comfort from the idea of a well-meaning but bumbling and inept deity, but I cannot find such a God in the pages of Scripture. The God portrayed there is the sovereign ruler of the universe. Nothing is impossible for him. He gathers the storm clouds and causes them to break with fury. He has all the stars numbered and named. He causes the light to dawn and the darkness to fall. He feeds the animals of the field, and he marks the sparrow's fall. He moves the hearts of kings to accomplish his will. No army marches on an enemy and no leaf trembles on a tree without God's knowledge and apart from his permission.

"Your God is my devil," is the slick response of some to the teaching of the sovereign God who brings difficulty into the lives of his people.

The Bible is clear about the reality of Satan. But it also will not let us get off the hook of suffering by hiding in the refuge of dualism: God and Satan are equal beings who are locked in combat with God winning some and the devil winning some.

Sure enough, Satan is present in the book of Job, but not as an equal with God. He has to ask God's permission before he can do anything to Job.

Job certainly was perplexed by the heavy doses of affliction that came his way, but he never for one moment doubted that they were from God. His suffering could not be explained in terms of an absentee God who had gone on vacation or was on sick leave. It was not the result of some cosmic malfunction. It did not catch God off guard, and it did not send heaven into a panic. Job had lots of questions about lots of things, but he never questioned whether his suffering came from God. He was sure of it.

And isn't it interesting that the book of Job does not conclude with an apology from God? It rather ends in a blaze of sovereignty that melts Job and leaves him speechless. The book ends with God on the throne and Job in the dust. God never explains Job's suffering. He essentially says: "I am God, and I do not owe you an explanation."

However we choose to explain our sufferings, the Bible will not allow us to explain them apart from the knowledge and purpose of the sovereign God. That door is not open to us because God did not intend for it to be.

Why does God tear?

God does indeed tear up the lives of his people from time to time. We are not allowed to cut the knot of suffering by denying the power of the sovereign God. But why does he tear? Is it because he does not truly love his people? Have we mistakenly attributed a loving nature to God? Are we to cut the knot of suffering by saying God does not care?

The same Scripture that will not allow us to explain suffering by denying the sovereignty of God closes this exit just as emphatically.

Our afflictions do not prove God to be unloving. They prove just the opposite. Parents should be able to understand this. Parenting requires us to discipline our children. That discipline may consist of us bringing some unpleasantness into their lives or withholding some good from them.

The child can find either form of discipline to be so very painful that he cries, but the parent refuses to remove the discipline. Why? Is it because the parent hates the child? To the contrary, the parent disciplines because he or she loves the child. The discipline is essential for the maturity of the child. Through it the parent is able to achieve things that he could never achieve without it.

God is ever the wise parent. As such, he disciplines his

children. He does not do so because he enjoys the pain of his children, but rather because he desires their progress.

My mess, his masterpiece

We all know that it's possible for two people to look at the same thing and draw quite different conclusions.

It is the same with God and us on this matter of him tearing up our lives. When God tore up my life, I saw a mess. But what did God see? What does he see when his people see only devastation?

We cannot answer this question until we nail down what God is doing in the lives of his people.

Much of our difficulty with God tearing us lies in our view of his purpose for our lives. We insist on making our own comfort and convenience God's major concern and purpose for our lives.

I have often put it in this way: If we begin with the wrong job description for God, he will always fail in our eyes.

If our job description for God is our comfort, anything that makes us uncomfortable automatically means he has failed. But what if that is not God's job description?

The fact is that we do not get to write God's job description. He has written his own, and it does not include anything about our comfort as his primary concern. What is God's job description? It is to seek the glory of His name.

This always bothers some. They think it is wrong for God to seek his own glory. If it is wrong for us to exalt ourselves, why is it not wrong for God to exalt himself? The answer is quite simple. God is an altogether different being. He is perfect, while we are imperfect. If as a perfect being, God did not seek his own glory, he would be imperfect!

One of the ways in which God glorifies himself is in making his people more like him. We can put it in this way: God is glorified through causing his people to be more and more conformed to the image of his Son.

While we think in terms of our comfort, God thinks in terms of our conformity! Conformity to the Lord Jesus!

Do we understand that with that conformity being God's primary purpose or goal for our lives that he has to go about things in an entirely different way than he would if his primary concern were our ease?

The story of Joseph

There was a time in which it must have appeared to Joseph as if God had made a mess out of his life. Hated by his brothers! Sold into slavery! Falsely accused and thrown into prison!

But Joseph's mess was God's masterpiece. God raised him from that prison, and made him second only to Pharaoh in the land of Egypt. From that position, he was able to save multitudes, including his own family, from the ravages of famine. Furthermore, God used Joseph to typify the Lord Jesus Christ, who suffered much at the hands of his kinsman so he could provide for his people by opening a far greater storehouse than Joseph opened.

When all the evidence was in, Joseph was able to say to his brothers: "You meant it for evil, but God meant it for good" (Gen. 50:10).

The mother eagle

We can also find insight into God's dealings with his children by considering the way in which the mother eagle treats her young:

> *As an eagle stirs up its nest,*
> *Hovers over its young,*
> *Spreading out its wings,*
> *taking them up,*
> *Carrying them on its wings,*
> *So the Lord alone led him,*
> *And there was no foreign god*
> *with him.*
> *(Deut. 32:11-12).*

At first glance, verse 11 seems to convey a very happy and tranquil picture. Here is the mother eagle tenderly caring for her young, and the little eaglets are happy and secure. But closer inspection reveals a far different picture. This verse tells us that the mother eagle "stirs up its nest." It further tells us that she carries her young on her wings.

Here, then, is the true picture. After several weeks of tender, loving care in which the mother eagle brings tasty morsels to the nest, her behaviour suddenly changes. She begins tearing the nest apart. She rips out the feathers. She breaks up the twigs. The eaglets are now frightened out of their wits. Why has their mother become so terrifying? The time has come for the eaglets to fly, and the mother knows that they will not attempt to do so as long as they can sit comfortably in the nest. So she begins to tear it apart.

With the nest all broken up and in disarray, the mother eagle is ready for the next step. She pushes one of the little eagles to the edge of what is left of the nest. He drops like a rock through the air, squawking as he falls. When it looks as if he will hit the ground, the mother swoops under him and catches him on her wings. After carrying him aloft, she tilts her wings and the eaglet falls again. But as he flaps his wings in fright, he now learns that he himself can fly.

If the mother eagle concerned herself with the short-term comfort of the little eagles, she would not tear up their nest and force them to fly. But she deliberately destroys their comfort because she has a more important and lasting benefit in mind. By teaching them to fly, she teaches them to provide for themselves.

God deals with us in like manner. We often want him to concern himself with our short-term comfort. We want him to make this day as easy and pleasurable as it can be. But he has a higher purpose in mind for us. He is concerned with our long-term good.

My tears in his bottle

Have you ever hit a snag in your reading of the Bible? You are gliding along with everything making perfect sense. Then you come across a phrase or verse that makes no sense at all. You've hit a snag.

Some years ago, I hit a snag in Psalm 56. It is a psalm in which David prays for God to grant him relief from oppressing, tormenting enemies who were hounding him "all day" (vv.1-2).

As he seeks God's help, he includes this petition: "Put my tears into Your bottle" (v. 8).

God putting our tears in his bottle! What does that mean? David was praying for God to preserve his tears. He wanted God to remember each one. But why? I would rather that God dry my tears now rather than remember them later.

Maybe David was finding relief in reminding himself that the tears of the child of God are never truly lost. There is a meaning behind them, and when we finally get to heaven, God will finally explain them all.

Trials dark on every hand
And we cannot understand
All the ways that God would lead us
To that blessed Promised Land.

But He'll guide us with his eye
And we'll follow till we die
And we'll understand it better
By and by.
—Charles A. Tindley

Yes, I find blessing in the same place David found it. It helps me to know that my tears are not meaningless, that God will remember them and explain them.

But as I reflected on God catching my tears in his bottle, I found even more blessing. Catching tears in a bottle is not something that can be done at a distance. This is close-up work. If God catches my tears in his bottle, he has to be very close to me indeed. He has not abandoned me.

The God whose tearing causes tears is near.

God's greatest tearing

God has done some real tearing through the centuries. He tore up the comfortable life of Abraham in Mesopotamia, and he tore up Jacob's life in Canaan. We have been reminded that God tore up the life of Joseph. To these we could add the names of Moses, Gideon, Ruth, David, Elijah, Jeremiah, Hosea, Daniel and Paul.

But God did his greatest tearing on a Roman cross outside Jerusalem more than two thousand years ago when Jesus died there. The core of the meaning of his death is found in his cry: "My God, My God, why have You forsaken Me?" (Matt. 27:46).

On the cross, God forsook God! God the Father forsook God the Son! The fellowship between Father and Son was torn. Why? The answer lies in the nature of what the Lord Jesus was doing on that cross. He was there to restore sinners to fellowship and friendship with God. There is only one way that sinners can have fellowship with God—sin must be taken out of the way. And there is only one way for sin to be taken out of the way—its price has to be paid. To say Jesus came to take sin out of the way so sinners could have fellowship with God is to say that he, Jesus, went to the cross to bear the penalty for their sins. Because the penalty of sin is eternal separation from God, to say Jesus that went to the cross to bear that penalty is to say that he went there to endure an eternity's worth of separation from God.

The greatest tearing God has ever done is when he tore the fellowship between himself and his Son so that believing sinners will never have to be torn from God for ever.

When God tears no more

I mentioned earlier that God is so near his suffering people that he can catch their tears in a bottle. There is much consolation in that, but there is even more in knowing that a day is coming in which the Lord will wipe the tears from the eyes of his people, and they will never weep again (Rev. 21:4).

One of my happiest memories is of my mother singing the great hymns of the faith during the years of my childhood. Here is one of her favorites:

Oft times the day seems long, our trials hard to bear,
We're tempted to complain, to murmur and despair;
But Christ will soon appear to catch His Bride away,
All tears forever over in God's eternal day.

Sometimes the sky looks dark with not a ray of light,
We're tossed and driven on, no human help in sight;
But there is one in heav'n who knows our deepest care,
Let Jesus solve your problem—just go to Him in pray'r.

Life's day will soon be o'er, all storms forever past,
We'll cross the great divide, to glory, safe at last;

We'll share the joys of heav'n—a harp, a home, a crown,
The tempter will be banished, we'll lay our burden down.

REFRAIN
It will be worth it all when we see Jesus,
Life's trials will seem so small when we see Christ;
One glimpse of His dear face all sorrow will erase,
So bravely run the race till we see Christ.
—Esther Kerr Rusthoi

When God tears up our lives, let's seek to remember that he always has our best interests in mind. He proved that at the cross! Let's also seek to remember that the tearing will be over when we get to heaven.

How much of life's race remains for me, I cannot say. But as I draw ever nearer the finish line, I look forward more and more to meeting the Lord Jesus Christ and to sharing his eternal glory. May the God of all grace help all who have read these chapters to desire nothing more than to be faithful to our great God and Saviour and to dread nothing more than dishonouring him.

Helpful resources on suffering

Behind a Frowning Providence, John J. Murray
The Hidden Smile of God, John Piper
The Mystery of Providence, John Flavel
Sickness and Death in the Christian Family, Peter Jeffrey

Sickness, Suffering and Scripture, David Leyshon

Spiritual Depression: Its Causes and Cure, D. Martyn Lloyd-Jones

Surprised by Suffering, R.C. Sproul

"Calvin did not invent a new teaching any more than Columbus invented America or Newton the law of gravity. As Columbus and Newton merely discovered what had existed all along, so Calvin uncovered truths that had been in the Bible all the time."[53]
—Edwin H. Palmer

"I believe that by my own reason or strength I cannot believe in Jesus Christ, my Lord, or come to him. But the Holy Spirit has called me through the Gospel, enlightened me with his gifts, and sanctified and preserved me in true faith."[54]
—Martin Luther

"We only use the term 'Calvinism' for shortness. That doctrine which is called 'Calvinism' did not spring from Calvin; we believe that it sprang from the great founder of all truth. … from Jesus Christ …."[55]
—Charles Spurgeon

12
"Are you a Calvinist?"

The religious context in which I came up taught that we are saved by grace through faith, which, of course, is exactly what the Bible affirms (Eph. 2:8-9). But the general understanding of this teaching was that God supplies the grace and we supply the faith. So salvation was a matter of God doing his part and we doing our part. God's part was, of course, to provide salvation through his Son, and our part is to receive the provision.

It was never openly admitted, but this teaching was another way of saying that part of the credit for our salvation goes to God and part of it goes to us. If someone is saved, it is due in part to him or her having enough good sense and courage to receive Christ. The person who does not receive Christ lacks these things. So the saved person deserves some credit for his salvation.

For several years I went along with this teaching, but something about it gnawed at me. If salvation is partly our work of faith did that not automatically cancel out God's grace? The apostle Paul plainly affirms that works and grace are mutually exclusive (Rom. 11:6). If salvation is a matter of grace, there is no place for works, and if it is a matter of works, there is no place for grace.

During those early years, I also found myself encountering Scriptures for which I had no category. I could not fit them into my system of doctrine. One such Scripture was Acts 13:48: "… as many as had been appointed to eternal life believed." But there were many, many others as well, some of which are: John 1:12-13; 6:37,39,44; 17:2; Acts 11:18; Rom. 8:29-30; 9:6-24; Eph. 2:1-10; Phil. 1:29; 1 Thess. 1:4; James 1:18; 1 Peter 1:2; 2 Peter 1:10-11.

During my university years, I encountered the teaching that is commonly called "Calvinism." This theological system advocated that salvation is entirely a matter of the grace of God. Even the faith with which we receive the gift is not something that we would generate if we could or could generate if we would. It is itself a gift of grace! So faith was not something for which we could take credit, and salvation was not part God's doing and part our doing. It was all God's doing! So all the glory for it properly goes to Him.

Early in my seminary career, I suspended my curiosity about Calvinism. The issue at that time was the reliability of Scripture. If the Bible was not the Word of God, it didn't matter what it had to say about salvation, or, for that matter, anything else! After I became convinced that the Bible is the inerrant, infallible Word of God, I again turned my attention to this question: What did the totally reliable Bible have to say about the way in which we are saved?

As I studied, I learned about the nature of man's sin problem. To put it mildly, I found that sin had radically damaged all of us. Man was made with a mind to understand God, with a heart to love God and with a will to choose God, but sin darkened our minds, degraded our affections and deadened our wills! Left to ourselves, we cannot understand the truth of God, we cannot love the things of God and we cannot choose the will of God. I came to understand that the depth of man's problem is not that he is sick and needs a little medicine but rather that he is dead and needs a resurrection! (Eph. 2:1).

A few years ago, one of my church members came storming into my study with these words: "I want to know straight out if you are a Calvinist." My answer to him was: "That depends on what you mean by the word 'Calvinist.'" It soon became clear that he regarded Calvinists as those who believe that there are people who want to be saved and God won't let them, and there are other people who don't want to be saved and God forces them! I assured him that I believe anyone can be saved who wants to be, but the problem is that no one left to himself wants to be saved (Rom. 3:11). It makes as much sense to talk about a mouse searching for a cat as it does to talk about a sinner searching for God!

It became clear to me that God did not have to do anything to save us. He could have left us in our sins and in our condemnation. But, wonder of wonders, God in grace chose a people for himself even before the world began! He determined that his Son would come into this world in their humanity and do for them everything necessary for them to be redeemed. The Lord Jesus was appointed as their surety, that is, as one who stands good for others. As their surety, he would render on their behalf the perfect obedience that God demanded, and he would bear the penalty for their sins.

God the Father also determined that his Holy Spirit would work in the hearts of those whom he, the Father, had chosen. The Holy Spirit would come into the spiritual cemetery, awaken them from the dead and grant them life. As a result of the work of the Holy Spirit, they would see the reality and gravity of their sins and the enormity of standing before God at the judgment. They would also see the sufficiency of the redeeming work of Christ and flee to him in true repentance and faith.

Those chosen by the Father, redeemed by the Son and regenerated by the Spirit, upon coming to faith, would begin to live to the honor and praise of the grace that had saved them. These would encounter many difficulties and challenges to their faith and would often fail, but the faith that the Spirit implanted in their hearts would never be uprooted. All who are saved will continue in the faith until they come home to heaven and receive the reward of faith.

When I came to this understanding of salvation, my heart was filled with awe and with joy. Salvation became to me the most wonderful thing imaginable.

My testimony is the same as many of those who have come to believe these things: the most difficult part is the proposition that Christ died only for those whom the Father had chosen. I was helped to some degree by various authors who affirmed that the atonement Jesus made was sufficient for all but efficient only for the elect.

But my reluctance finally melted when I began to grapple with the nature of what Christ did on the cross. I had long held to the substitutionary view of the atonement, but I had not thought it through. It occurred to me that the nature of the atonement determines its scope. If Jesus' death was substitutionary, it means that he took the place of sinners and received the penalty that their sins deserved. It means Jesus actually experienced hell on the cross!

Now if Jesus died for all without exception, he went to hell for all without exception! If we say, then, that Jesus died for people who will eventually end up in hell, we essentially accuse God of being unjust. He exacted the penalty for sinners from Jesus and will exact the same penalty from sinners who do not believe in Jesus. God would then be twice exacting the penalty for the same offense!

When we get to the nub of the matter, there are only three possibilities on the matter of the atonement. We can say that Christ received the penalty for all, so all must be saved (including those who never believe in him). Or we can say that Christ received the penalty for all, but only some will be saved (making God unjust). Or we can say that Christ received the penalty for some and those alone will be saved.

I have no particular liking for the label "Calvinism," but I do believe that the doctrines associated with that label are indeed taught by Scripture. I also sympathize with those who struggle with these matters. One who struggled as much as I did cannot help but sympathize. I would only ask my anti-Calvinistic friends to think seriously and deeply about certain questions. What does the word "grace" mean? How much credit does God deserve for the salvation of his people? Do we give him the glory for it or reserve part of it for ourselves? What did Paul mean when he told the Ephesians that they were chosen in Christ before the foundation of the world? (Eph. 1:4). If election is only a matter of God choosing in advance those whom he knew would choose him, why would this cause men to "reply against God"? (Rom. 9:20). If man's will is free, why does Paul tell us that no one seeks after God? (Rom. 3:11). If sinners are saved by exercising their free wills, why does the Bible tell us that spiritual birth is not due to the will of man, but of God? (John 1:13). If we have something to do with our regeneration, why does the Bible use the emblem of birth to depict it? To put it another way—if we contributed nothing to our physical birth, why do we insist that we contribute something to spiritual birth? If we do not object to God's choosing of Israelites in the Old Testament era, why object to the New Testament's teaching on election? What does a substitutionary atonement mean?

My teaching on God's saving grace has caused some to ask: "Do we not contribute anything at all to our salvation?" I always answer by saying: "There is only one thing—sin!"

Some insist that the doctrine of salvation by grace cuts the nerve of evangelism. They contend that there is no need to witness, preach, pray or give if Calvinism is true! But the very same God who saves sinners has determined that he will save them through his people spreading his gospel! The truth is the doctrines of grace do not kill evangelism but enliven and promote it. Think of it in this way: would we be more inclined to go into a field to look for diamonds if we did not know whether any were there? Or would we be more inclined to go if we knew for sure that diamonds were there in abundance? The answer is obvious! God's plan of grace assures us that there are diamonds in the field! Therefore, wc can go about the work of evangelism with the confident assurance that the Lord will actually use our efforts to bring people to Christ. While engaged in ministry in Corinth, Paul received the assurance that the Lord had many people there even before they became his people! (Acts 18:9-10).

I expect to be surprised by many things in heaven, but I will not be surprised at all when the God of all grace makes it indisputably clear that the salvation of his people was entirely a matter of his grace. But the fact that I will not be surprised does not mean that I will not be lost in wonder, love and praise.

Helpful resources on Calvinism

A Journey in Grace, Richard Belcher

By His Grace and for His Glory, Tom Nettles

Chosen by God, R.C. Sproul

Evangelistic Calvinism, John Benton

Five Points of Calvinism, W.J. Seaton

The Five Points of Calvinism, David N. Steele, Curtis C. Thomas, S. Lance Quinn

Grace Unknown, R.C. Sproul

Spurgeon versus Hyper-Calvinism, Iain Murray

The Doctrines of Grace, James M. Boice and Philip Graham Ryken

The Reformed Doctrine of Predestination, Lorraine Boettner

The Sovereignty of Grace, Arthur Custance

The Reign of Grace, Abraham Booth

What is a True Calvinist? Philip Graham Ryken

What are Election and Predestination? Richard Phillips

Who Saves, God or Me? Erroll Hulse

Whatever Happened to the Gospel of Grace? James Montgomery Boice

Willing to Believe, R.C. Sproul

"As for myself, I am compelled to say with solemn truthfulness that I am not content with anything I have ever done. … Whatever grace has done for me I acknowledge with deep gratitude; but so far as I have done anything myself I beg pardon for it. I pray God to forgive my prayers, for they have been full of fault; I beseech him to forgive even this confession, for it is not as humble as it ought to be; I beseech him to wash my tears and purge my devotions, and to baptize me into a true burial with my Savior, that I may be quite forgotten in myself, and only remembered in him."[56]

—Charles Spurgeon

Books by Roger Ellsworth

Come Down Lord! The Banner of Truth Trust

Is There An Answer? The Banner of Truth Trust

Standing for God (The Life of Elijah), The Banner of Truth Trust

Strengthening Christ's Church (1 Corinthians), Evangelical Press

Faithful under Fire (The Life of Joseph), Evangelical Press

Journey to the Cross, Evangelical Press

A Promise is a Promise, Evangelical Press

He is Altogether Lovely (The Song of Solomon), Evangelical Press

The Shepherd King (The Life of David), Evangelical Press

How to Live in a Dangerous World, Evangelical Press

31 Days of Christmas, Evangelical Press

Special Sermons for Special Days, Loizeau Publications

From Glory to Ruin (1 Kings), Evangelical Press

Apostasy, Destruction and Hope (2 Kings), Evangelical Press

The Bible Book by Book, Evangelical Press

Be Patient! God Hasn't Finished with Me Yet! (The Life of Jacob), Evangelical Press

The Guide to Christian Comfort, Evangelical Press

The God of All Comfort (Isaiah 40-66), Evangelical Press

Opening up Philippians, Day One Publications

Opening up Psalms, Day One Publications

Opening up Malachi, Day One Publications

Moses: God's Man for Challenging Times, Evangelical Press

Hold Your Course: 22 Daily Readings from Colossians, Evangelical Press

What the Bible Teaches about Angels, Evangelical Press

What the Bible Teaches about Christian Parenting, Evangelical Press

Face2Face with Samuel, Day One Publications

Face2Face with Simon Peter, Day One Publications

People in the Passion of Jesus, Day One Publications

What the Bible Teaches about Heaven, Evangelical Press

They Echoed the Voice of God, Day One Publications

When Heaven Calls Your Name, Day One Publications

Opening up Joshua, Day One Publications

Opening up James, Day One Publications

31 Great Chapters of the Old Testament, Evangelical Press

Foundations for the Faith (The Gospel of John), Evangelical Press

When God Makes Streams in the Desert, Day One Publications

Exploring the Fascinating Life of Jesus, Evangelical Press

Endnotes

[1] J.I. Packer, *Collected Shorter Writings of J.I. Packer: Honouring the Written Word of God*, (Cumbria: Paternoster Press, 1999), vol. iii, p.264.

[2] F.B. Meyer, cited by Derek Prime and Alistair Begg, *On Being a Pastor*, (Chicago: Moody Publishers, 2004), p.17.

[3] Adrian Rogers, *Standing for Light and Truth* (Wheaton, IL, Crossway Books, 2003), p.69.

[4] cited by Peter Barnes, *A Handful of Pebbles* (Edinburgh: The Banner of Truth Trust, 2008), p.81.

[5] Packer, *Collected Shorter Writings*, vol. iii, p.282.

[6] D. Martyn Lloyd-Jones, *God's Way of Reconciliation* (Grand Rapids: Baker Book House, 1972), p.59.

[7]A.W. Pink, *Gleanings in Genesis*, (Chicago: Moody Press, 1922), p.20.

[8] S.G. DeGraaf, *Promise and Deliverance* (Ontario: Paideia Press, 1977), vol. i, p.21.

[9] Ibid., p.22.

[10] Ibid., p.19.

[11] Rogers, *Standing for Light*, p.149

[12] Peter Jeffrey, *Believers Need the Gospel*, (Amityville, NY: Calvary Press, 2000), p.8.

[13] cited by Gary Gilley, *This Little Church Went to Market* (Durham: Evangelical Press, 2005), p.83.

[14] cited by Iain Murray, *The Forgotten Spurgeon* (Edinburgh: The Banner of Truth Trust, 1966), p.208.

[15] T. David Gordon, *Why Johnny Can't Preach*, Phillipsburg, New Jersey: P&R Publishing, 2009), pp.58-9.

[16] John R.W. Stott, *God's Book for God's People* (Downer's Grove, IL: InterVarsity Press, 1982), p.1.

[17] Steven J. Lawson, *Famine in the Land*, (Chicago: Moody Press, 2003), p.94.

[18] Josh McDowell, *The New Evidence That Demands a Verdict* (Nashville: Thomas Nelson Publishers, 1999), p.168.

[19] D. James Kennedy, *Why I Believe* (Nashville: Word Publishing, 1980), p.47.

[20] cited by Josh McDowell, *The New Evidence*, p.11

[21] cited by W.A. Criswell, *Why I Preach the Bible is Literally True*, (Nashville: Broadman Press, 1969), p.45.

[22] website, *Sermons on several occasions* – Google Books.

[23] cited by Lawson, *Famine,* p.24.

[24] J.I. Packer, "Why Preach?" in *The Preacher and Preaching*, Samuel T. Logan, Jr., ed. (Phillipsburg: Presbyterian and Reformed Publishing Company, 1986), p.20.

[25] John R.W. Stott, *Between Two Worlds* (Grand Rapids: William B. Eerdmans Publishing Company, 1982), p.113.

[26] As above, p.109.

[27] Packer, *Collected Writings*, vol.iii, p.278.

[28] Stott, *Between Two Worlds*, p.264.

[29] W. Robert Godfrey, *An Unexpected Journey* (Phillipsburg: P&R Publishing, 2004), p.37

[30] Joel R. Beeke, *Puritan Reformed Spirituality*, (Grand Rapids: Reformation Heritage Books, 2004), p.434.

[31] cited by Stott, *Between Two Worlds*, pp.151-2.

[32] John Piper, *The Supremacy of God in Preaching* (Grand Rapids: Baker Book House, 1990), p.9.

[33] As above, p.55.

[34] cited by Lawson, *Famine*, p.56.

[35] Stott, *Between Two Worlds*, pp.278-9.

[36] As above, p.284.

[37] cited by Gilley, *This Little Church*, p.31

[38] R.C. Sproul, "The Teaching Preacher," in *Feed My Sheep* (Morgan, PA, Soli Deo Gloria Publications, 2002), p.155.

[39] cited by Gilley, *This Little Church*, p.68.

[40] An interview with Michael Horton, *The Discerning Reader* (Grand Rapids: Baker Book House Company, no date), no.8, p.4.

[41] Stott, *Between Two Worlds*, p.52.

[42] Piper, *Supremacy*, pp.55-6.

[43] As above, p.57.

[44] *A Puritan Golden Treasury*, compiled by I.D.E. Thomas, (Edinburgh, The

Banner of Truth Trust, 1977), p.223.

[45] Brian H. Edwards, *Revival! A people saturated with God* (Durham, Evangelical Press, 1990), pp.28-29.

[46] Arnold Dallimore, *George Whitefield* (Westchester, IL: Cornerstone Books, 1979), vol. i, pp.25-6.

[47] As above, p.31.

[48] As above.

[49] As above.

[50] Iain Murray, *Jonathan Edwards: A New Biography* (Edinburgh: The Banner of Truth Trust, 1987), p.159.

[51] Dallimore, *George Whitefield*, vol. i, p.32.

[52] Edwards, *Revival!*, pp.271-75.

[53] cited by Steven J. Lawson, *Foundations of Grace* (Orlando: Reformation Trust Publishing, 2006), vol. i, p.306.

[54] cited by Steven J. Lawson, *Foundations of Grace*, p.186.

[55] *C.H. Spurgeon Autobiography* (Edinburgh: The Banner of Truth Trust, 1981), vol. i, p.162.

[56] Spurgeon, *Autobiography*, vol. ii, p.v.

About the Author

Roger Ellsworth has spent fifty years of his life preaching the Gospel of Jesus Christ. He is a pastor and the author of numerous books including his contributions to the Welwyn Commentary Series.